FOR THE LOVE OF SPORTS
PICKLEBALL

Yolanda Ridge

www.openlightbox.com

Step 1
Go to www.openlightbox.com

Step 2
Enter this unique code

DQPGE1IKZ

Step 3
Explore your interactive eBook!

CONTENTS
- 4 What Is Pickleball?
- 6 Getting Ready to Play
- 8 The Pickleball Court
- 9 USA Pickleball Nationals
- 10 Keeping Score
- 12 Rules of the Court
- 14 Playing the Game
- 16 History of Pickleball
- 18 Superstars of Pickleball
- 20 Staying Healthy
- 22 The Pickleball Quiz

AV2 is optimized for use on any device

Your interactive eBook comes with...

Contents — Browse a live contents page to easily navigate through resources

Audio — Listen to sections of the book read aloud

Videos — Watch informative video clips

Weblinks — Gain additional information for research

Slideshows — View images and captions

Try This! — Complete activities and hands-on experiments

Key Words — Study vocabulary, and complete a matching word activity

Quizzes — Test your knowledge

Share — Share titles within your Learning Management System (LMS) or Library Circulation System

Citation — Create bibliographical references following APA, CMOS, and MLA styles

This title is part of our AV2 digital subscription

1-Year Grades K–5 Subscription
ISBN 978-1-7911-3320-7

Access hundreds of AV2 titles with our digital subscription.
Sign up for a FREE trial at www.openlightbox.com/trial

FOR THE LOVE OF SPORTS
PICKLEBALL

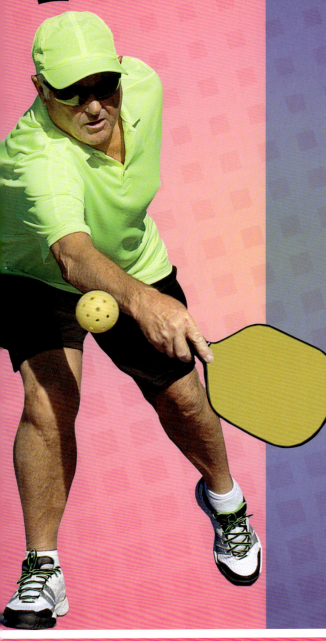

CONTENTS

- 2   Interactive eBook Code
- 4   What Is Pickleball?
- 6   Getting Ready to Play
- 8   The Pickleball Court
- 9   USA Pickleball Nationals
- 10 Keeping Score
- 12 Rules of the Court
- 14 Playing the Game
- 16 History of Pickleball
- 18 Superstars of Pickleball
- 20 Staying Healthy
- 22 The Pickleball Quiz
- 23 Key Words/Index

What Is Pickleball?

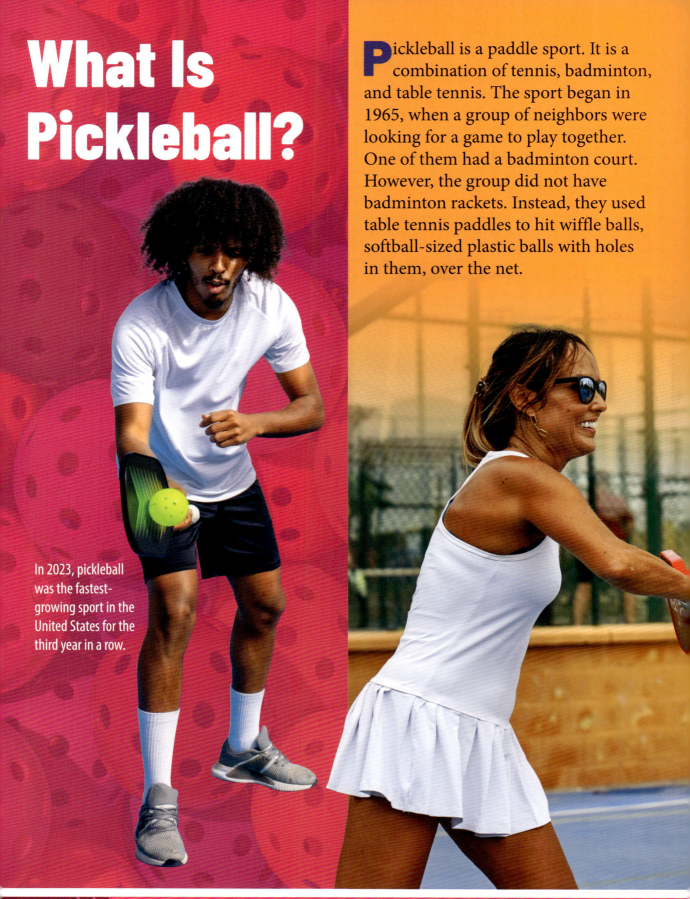

Pickleball is a paddle sport. It is a combination of tennis, badminton, and table tennis. The sport began in 1965, when a group of neighbors were looking for a game to play together. One of them had a badminton court. However, the group did not have badminton rackets. Instead, they used table tennis paddles to hit wiffle balls, softball-sized plastic balls with holes in them, over the net.

In 2023, pickleball was the fastest-growing sport in the United States for the third year in a row.

As the neighbors played, they found that the ball bounced well off the hard surface of the badminton court. They later lowered the badminton net to about the height of a tennis net. They also began to modify their equipment. After a few years, a full set of rules for the new game was developed.

The first pickleball **tournaments** were organized in Washington in 1982. Within 20 years, the sport was being played in all 50 states. Today, the sport's popularity is spreading around the world.

Doubles pickleball matches are played between two-player teams.

Pickleball was named the official state sport of Washington in 2022.

Sixty countries belong to the World Pickleball Federation.

The average age of a pickleball player is 35.

Pickleball 5

Getting Ready to Play

A pickleball is 2.9 to 3 inches (7.4 to 7.6 centimeters) across and weighs between 0.8 and 1 ounces (22.7 and 28.4 grams).

Playing pickleball requires a net, a ball, and one paddle for each player. Pickleball paddles have a solid, smooth surface. They were originally made of wood. In 1984, airplane engineer Arlen Paranto invented the first non-wooden pickleball paddle, using the same material found inside aircraft. It was much lighter than the wooden ones.

A pickleball is usually made of hard, smooth plastic. The hollow ball has between 26 and 40 holes drilled into it. Pickleballs come in many different colors. Bright yellow is the most common.

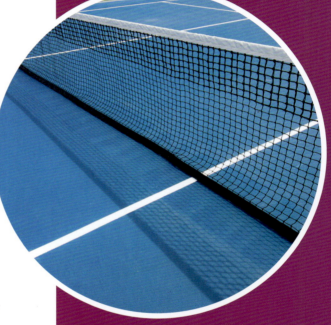

The pickleball net is 36 inches (91.4 cm) high at the posts and 34 inches (86.4 cm) high at the center.

A pair of court shoes with rubber **soles** helps players make quick movements and shift from side to side.

6 For the Love of Sports

There is no **dress code** for pickleball. However, experts suggest wearing comfortable, stretchy clothes that allow a player to move easily.

Pickleball paddles cannot be longer than 17 inches (43.2 cm). They are usually between 7 and 8 inches (17.8 and 20.3 cm) wide.

Shorts or skirts with pockets make it easy to carry an extra ball around the court.

Pickleball 7

The Pickleball Court

An official pickleball court is the same size as a badminton court. This means that four pickleball courts take up the same space as one tennis court. Pickleball courts have a hard surface, usually concrete or asphalt.

Boundary lines around a pickleball court show the play area. These lines are called baselines and sidelines. To score a point, the ball must land on or inside the lines.

The net runs across the middle of the court, halfway between the baselines. A non-**volley** line runs on either side of the net, in the same direction as the baseline. The area between these non-volley lines is known as the **kitchen**. A service centerline runs down the middle of the court, from the non-volley line to the baseline.

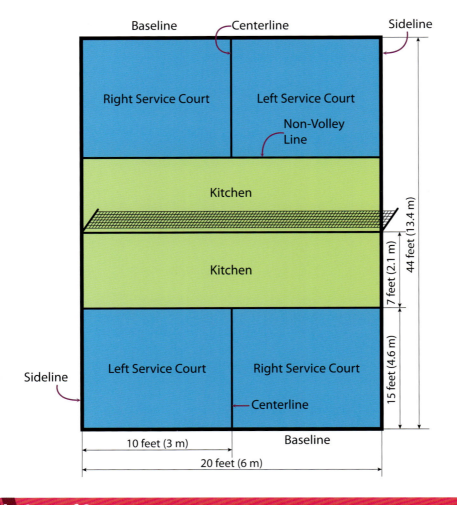

8   For the Love of Sports

USA Pickleball Nationals

The first USA Pickleball National Championships were held in Buckeye, Arizona, in 2009. It had just under 400 participants. People from 26 states and several Canadian provinces competed. The event has grown rapidly since that time. In 2023, about 50,000 spectators went to the Nationals in Dallas, Texas.

Dallas, Texas
The 2023 USA Pickleball Nationals were held at Brookhaven Country Club, in Farmers Branch, part of Dallas, Texas. More than 2.6 million television viewers watched 6,928 matches. It was the biggest event in the history of the sport.

Keeping Score

Recreational pickleball is usually played between teams of two. Singles pickleball is less common. In doubles, the teams decide who goes first randomly, using methods such as tossing a coin or spinning a paddle. The player on the right side of the court **serves** the ball from behind the baseline. The ball must go across the court diagonally and bounce beyond the non-volley line.

Points can only be scored by the serving team. If the receiving team cannot return the serve or **rally**, the serving team earns a point. Games are usually played to 11 points. However, the winning team must also have two more points than their opponents, so some games will be played to a higher point total.

In the ready position, players keep their paddles up and their legs bent. It is best to stay behind the ball and use short back swings.

10 For the Love of Sports

The player receiving the serve must let the ball bounce once before hitting it back. If the ball bounces twice, gets hit out of bounds, or does not go over the net, the rally is finished. If the serving team wins a point, the server goes to the other service court on their side of the net to serve again. If not, the other player on the serving team has a chance to serve.

Once both team members have lost a rally on their serve, the other team gets to serve.

In doubles games, the team that goes first can only lose one rally before the other team serves. After this, both teams are allowed to lose two rallies before switching which team serves.

Pickleball 11

Rules of the Court

As the ball must bounce before the receiving team can return the serve, pickleball is said to have a two-bounce rule. The rule also means the ball must bounce before the serving team hits the return. After the first two hits, the ball no longer needs to bounce before it can be returned.

Another pickleball rule is "no volleys in the kitchen." Players cannot hit the ball out of the air when standing in the area between the non-volley line and the net. However, reaching over the non-volley line to hit the ball is allowed. Players can also hit the ball after it bounces in the kitchen.

Players can stand anywhere on their side of the court. This includes the kitchen, as long as the player does not volley the ball while there. The general strategy is to move close to the non-volley line after the ball has been served and received.

Typically, the serving player must state the score before each serve. However, in a tournament, the referee will do this.

12 For the Love of Sports

Faults occur when a player violates the two-bounce rule or volleys while in the kitchen. If any part of a player's body or paddle touches the pickleball net or posts, it is also a fault. If the serving team commits a fault, they lose a serve. If the receiving team commits a fault, the serving team gets a point.

Hitting the ball out of bounds or into the net is considered a type of fault.

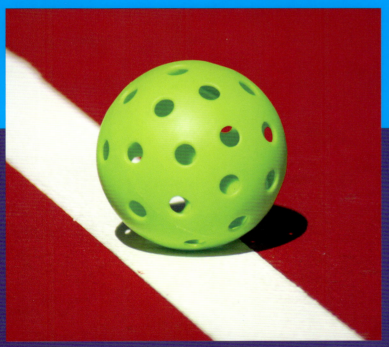

If a ball hits any part of the boundary line, it is considered in. The team on that side of the net should clearly call "in" or "out" after the ball lands and the play ends.

Pickleball 13

Playing the Game

Many people play pickleball simply for fun. Recreational pickleball often focuses on the social elements of the sport. The environment is supportive and inviting. Some recreational leagues are split by skill level, but many are open to all players. In recent years, recreational courts have been built in places such as community centers and retirement complexes due to the sport's popularity across age groups. Many colleges have pickleball clubs, too.

Pickleball can be played indoors or outdoors. In some places, tennis courts have been converted into pickleball courts.

Para pickleball is a slightly modified version of the sport. It is played by people in wheelchairs.

Several major pickleball tournaments are held around the world every year. The top competitions in the United States are the USA Pickleball National Championships and the US Open Pickleball Championships. Both tournaments feature multiple events. These include men's and women's singles and doubles competitions. There are also mixed doubles competitions, where each team has one woman and one man.

The Association of Pickleball **Professionals** (APP) and the Professional Pickleball Association organize events and provide player rankings. One way to enter Major League Pickleball is through success in Minor League Pickleball. While most popular in its country of origin, pickleball is played all across the world. The largest pickleball tournament outside of the United States is the English Open. In 2024, it had nearly 2,000 competitors from 45 countries.

The United States, Canada, India, and Spain were original members of the International Pickleball Federation, which, at that time, was called the International Federation of Pickleball.

The International Pickleball Federation's main event is the Bainbridge Cup tournament. It is named after the place in which pickleball was invented. The tournament is open to **amateur** and professional players alike.

Pickleball 15

History of Pickleball

Pickleball was named after a "pickle boat." This name is often used for a boat rowed by crew members from different teams for fun after a race. Pickleball reminded Joan Pritchard, one of the game's creators, of a pickle boat because it is a mixture of different sports.

On October 10, 2021, in celebration of World Pickleball Day, Angelo A. Rossetti and Ettore Rossetti achieved a world record for the longest pickleball rally. The brothers hit the ball back and forth 16,046 times.

1965 Pickleball is invented by a group of neighbors on Bainbridge Island, near Seattle, Washington.

1976 The first pickleball tournament in the world is held at South Center Athletic Club, in Tukwila, Washington.

1984 The United States Amateur Pickleball Association is organized. It creates the first official pickleball rulebook.

2005 The USA Pickleball Association is formed. Renamed USA Pickleball (USAP) in 2020, it is the national governing body for the sport in the United States, providing official rules, tournaments, and rankings.

2010 What is now the International Pickleball Federation is developed to help grow the sport around the world.

2023 The APP releases a report stating that more than 14 percent of U.S. adults had played pickleball at least once in the previous year.

World Pickleball Day, introduced by the World Pickleball Federation, was celebrated for the first time in 2020.

In 2001, pickleball was introduced as a demonstration sport in the Arizona Senior Olympics.

Three to six people have been inducted into the Pickleball Hall of Fame every year since 2017.

Pickleball 17

Superstars of Pickleball

Pickleball greats from all over the world inspire players to take up the sport.

Billy J. Jacobsen
BIRTH DATE: October 15, 1962
HOMETOWN: Seattle, Washington

CAREER FACTS:
- Billy played pickleball for more than 34 years and introduced several new rules to the sport.
- Every year from 1981 to 2008, Billy won at least one tournament in either doubles, mixed doubles, or singles.
- Billy is one of very few players to win open singles and open doubles tournaments using only his left or only his right hand for the entire event.
- During his career, Billy's record included more than 50 medals in Open Men's Singles and Doubles.
- Billy was inducted into the Pickleball Hall of Fame in 2017.

Daniel Gabanek
BIRTH DATE: November 8, 1963
HOMETOWN: Bratislava, Slovakia

CAREER FACTS:
- Daniel played his first tournament in January 1986 at an event organized by pickleball pioneer Sid Williams.
- From 1988 to 2014, Daniel won 21 gold medals in men's singles competitions.
- Daniel has 60 gold medals in men's doubles and 13 in Open Mixed Doubles.
- In 2019, Daniel was inducted into the Pickleball Hall of Fame.

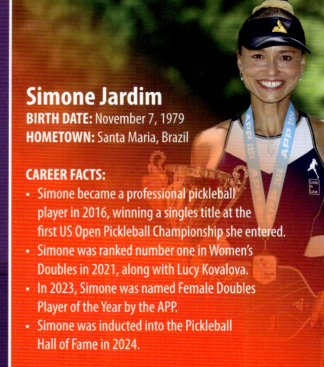

Simone Jardim
BIRTH DATE: November 7, 1979
HOMETOWN: Santa Maria, Brazil

CAREER FACTS:
- Simone became a professional pickleball player in 2016, winning a singles title at the first US Open Pickleball Championship she entered.
- Simone was ranked number one in Women's Doubles in 2021, along with Lucy Kovalova.
- In 2023, Simone was named Female Doubles Player of the Year by the APP.
- Simone was inducted into the Pickleball Hall of Fame in 2024.

Catherine Parenteau
BIRTH DATE: August 26, 1994
HOMETOWN: Montreal, Quebec, Canada

CAREER FACTS:
- Catherine was introduced to pickleball in 2015 by Simone Jardim, who was her tennis coach. After only six months, she entered her first US Open and won in a mixed bracket.
- Catherine won the 2021 US Open Pro Women's Doubles title with partner, Callie Smith.
- Catherine has been ranked as high as number two in women's singles and women's doubles.

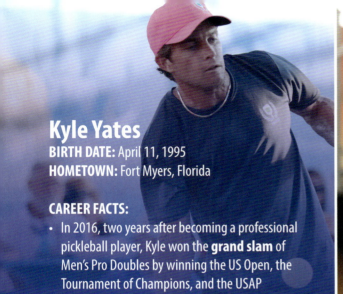

Kyle Yates
BIRTH DATE: April 11, 1995
HOMETOWN: Fort Myers, Florida

CAREER FACTS:
- In 2016, two years after becoming a professional pickleball player, Kyle won the **grand slam** of Men's Pro Doubles by winning the US Open, the Tournament of Champions, and the USAP National Championships.
- Kyle won US Open titles for Mixed Pros Doubles with Simone Jardim in 2018 and 2019.

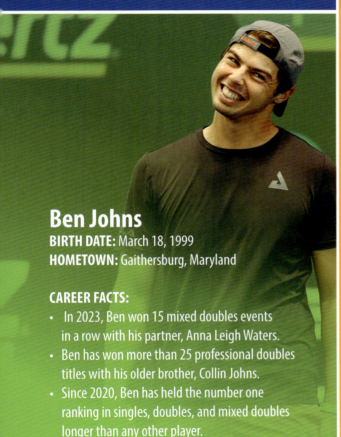

Ben Johns
BIRTH DATE: March 18, 1999
HOMETOWN: Gaithersburg, Maryland

CAREER FACTS:
- In 2023, Ben won 15 mixed doubles events in a row with his partner, Anna Leigh Waters.
- Ben has won more than 25 professional doubles titles with his older brother, Collin Johns.
- Since 2020, Ben has held the number one ranking in singles, doubles, and mixed doubles longer than any other player.
- Considered by many to be the greatest pickleball player of all time, Ben has about 100 titles more than any other male player.

Anna Leigh Waters
BIRTH DATE: January 26, 2007
HOMETOWN: Delray Beach, Florida

CAREER FACTS:
- When Anna Leigh was 12 years old, she became the youngest professional pickleball player in history.
- Anna Leigh won her first national title in the Women's Doubles Pro category at the 2019 US Open Pickleball Championships, where she partnered with her mother.
- From 2022 to 2024, Anna Leigh was the Professional Pickleball Association's number one ranked player in singles, doubles, and mixed doubles.
- Anna Leigh was the worlds' highest-paid pickleball player in 2024.

Pickleball

Staying Healthy

Pickleball is a healthy activity for people of all ages and skill levels. It provides exercise and social interaction. Like other sports, it is important to drink water while playing. This replaces fluid lost through sweat. Eating a well-balanced diet also helps athletes stay in shape. Fruits and vegetables provide necessary vitamins and minerals. Breads, pasta, and rice are sources of energy. Protein-rich foods, such as eggs, tofu, and fish, help build and repair muscles and bones.

Pickleball instructors are certified through organizations such as the International Pickleball Teaching Professional Association and Pickleball Coaching International.

The "no volleys in the kitchen" rule makes the game safer for everyone. The non-volley zone prevents players from charging the net and smashing the ball into an opponent.

Pickleball **warmup** activities prepare the body for game play. An easy jog can get the heart rate up and activate the muscles. Shoulder circles and trunk twists loosen up the joints. Side hops and lunges prepare the hips, legs, and ankles for side-to-side movement on the court.

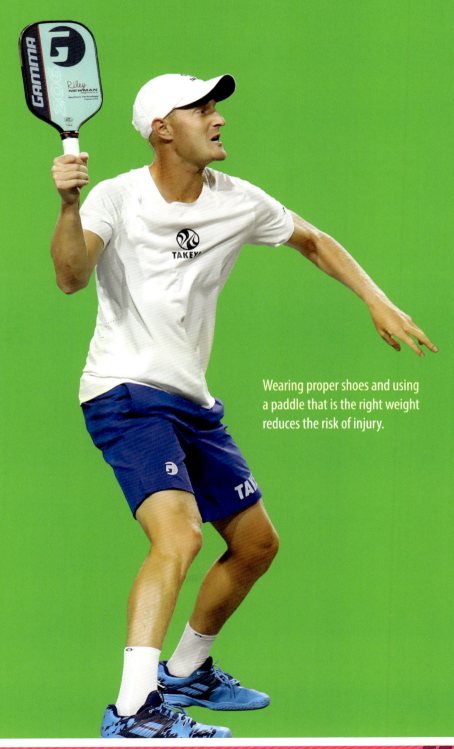

Wearing proper shoes and using a paddle that is the right weight reduces the risk of injury.

Pickleball 21

THE PICKLEBALL QUIZ

- 1 - Pickleball is a combination of which **three** sports?

- 2 - In what year was **pickleball** invented?

- 3 - Pickleball is the **official sport** of which American state?

- 4 - What is not allowed in the **kitchen**?

- 5 - In which year were the first **USA Pickleball National Championships** held?

- 6 - What type of **shoe** is best for pickleball?

- 7 - How high is a **pickleball net** at the posts?

- 8 - In which year was **World Pickleball Day** introduced?

- 9 - Who has won at least **100 more titles** than any other male pickleball player?

- 10 - Who was the world's **highest-paid** pickleball player in 2024?

ANSWERS: **1** Badminton, tennis, and table tennis; **2** 1965; **3** Washington; **4** Volleying; **5** 2009; **6** Court shoes with rubber soles; **7** 36 inches (91 cm); **8** 2020; **9** Ben Johns; **10** Anna Leigh Waters

22 For the Love of Sports

Key Words

amateur: a person who is not paid to play a game and who may not have much experience

boundary: the outer border or edges of something

dress code: clothing that must be worn in order to take part in an event

grand slam: to win all of the major tournaments in a sport in the same year

kitchen: the area in a pickleball court between the non-volley line and the net

professionals: also known as pros, people who are paid to play a sport

rally: in pickleball, a continuous back and forth of the ball between the serving and receiving team

recreational: an activity that is done for fun

serves: puts the ball in play by hitting it

soles: the parts of shoes that make contact with the ground

tournaments: competitions in which contestants play a series of games to decide the winner

volley: in pickleball, to hit the ball out of the air before it has bounced on the ground

warmup: gentle exercises that prepare a person's body for game play

Index

Association of Pickleball Professionals (APP) 15, 17, 18

Gabanek, Daniel 18

International Pickleball Federation 15, 17
International Pickleball Teaching Professional Association 20

Jacobsen, Billy J. 18
Jardim, Simone 18, 19
Johns, Ben 19, 22
Johns, Collin 19

Kovalova, Lucy 18

Major League Pickleball 15
Minor League Pickleball 15

Paranto, Arlen 6
Parenteau, Catherine 18
Pickleball Coaching International 20
Professional Pickleball Association 15, 19

Smith, Callie 18

USA Pickleball (USAP) 5, 17, 19
USA Pickleball National Championships 9, 15, 19, 22
US Open Pickleball Championships 15, 18, 19

Waters, Anna Leigh 19, 22
Williams, Sid 18
World Pickleball Day 16, 17, 22
World Pickleball Federation 5, 17

Yates, Kyle 19

Get the best of both worlds.

AV2 bridges the gap between print and digital.

The expandable resources toolbar enables quick access to content including videos, audio, activities, **weblinks**, **slideshows**, **quizzes**, and **key words**.

Animated videos make static images come alive.

Resource icons on each page help readers to further **explore key concepts**.

Published by Lightbox Learning Inc.
276 5th Avenue, Suite 704 #917
New York, NY 10001
Website: www.openlightbox.com

Copyright ©2026 Lightbox Learning Inc.
All rights reserved. No part of this publication may be reproduced, stored in a retrieval system, or transmitted in any form or by any means, electronic, mechanical, photocopying, recording, or otherwise, without the prior written permission of the publisher.

Library of Congress Control Number: 2025931413

ISBN 979-8-8745-2543-9 (hardcover)
ISBN 979-8-8745-2544-6 (softcover)
ISBN 979-8-8745-2545-3 (static multi-user eBook)
ISBN 979-8-8745-2547-7 (interactive multi-user eBook)

Printed in Guangzhou, China
1 2 3 4 5 6 7 8 9 0 29 28 27 26 25

012025
101124

Project Coordinator John Willis
Art Director Terry Paulhus
Layout Jean Faye Rodriguez

Photo Credits
Every reasonable effort has been made to trace ownership and to obtain permission to reprint copyright material. The publisher would be pleased to have any errors or omissions brought to its attention so that they may be corrected in subsequent printings. The publisher acknowledges Alamy, Getty Images, Shutterstock, and Wikimedia as its primary image suppliers for this title.

View new titles and product videos at www.openlightbox.com